YOUR KNOWLEDGE HAS VALUE

Philip Diego

Business Strategy

GRIN Verlag

Bibliografische Information der Deutschen Nationalbibliothek:

Die Deutsche Bibliothek verzeichnet diese Publikation in der Deutschen National-
bibliografie; detaillierte bibliografische Daten sind im Internet über http://dnb.d-
nb.de/ abrufbar.

Dieses Werk sowie alle darin enthaltenen einzelnen Beiträge und Abbildungen
sind urheberrechtlich geschützt. Jede Verwertung, die nicht ausdrücklich vom
Urheberrechtsschutz zugelassen ist, bedarf der vorherigen Zustimmung des Verla-
ges. Das gilt insbesondere für Vervielfältigungen, Bearbeitungen, Übersetzungen,
Mikroverfilmungen, Auswertungen durch Datenbanken und für die Einspeicherung
und Verarbeitung in elektronische Systeme. Alle Rechte, auch die des auszugsweisen
Nachdrucks, der fotomechanischen Wiedergabe (einschließlich Mikrokopie) sowie
der Auswertung durch Datenbanken oder ähnliche Einrichtungen, vorbehalten.

Imprint:

Copyright © 2013 GRIN Verlag GmbH
Druck und Bindung: Books on Demand GmbH, Norderstedt Germany
ISBN: 978-3-656-63751-6

This book at GRIN:

http://www.grin.com/en/e-book/271574/business-strategy

GRIN - Your knowledge has value

Der GRIN Verlag publiziert seit 1998 wissenschaftliche Arbeiten von Studenten, Hochschullehrern und anderen Akademikern als eBook und gedrucktes Buch. Die Verlagswebsite www.grin.com ist die ideale Plattform zur Veröffentlichung von Hausarbeiten, Abschlussarbeiten, wissenschaftlichen Aufsätzen, Dissertationen und Fachbüchern.

Visit us on the internet:

http://www.grin.com/

http://www.facebook.com/grincom

http://www.twitter.com/grin_com

Business strategy

Business strategy can be defined in various ways. According to the oxford dictionary, it is a plan designed for a particular purpose. It can also be viewed as the direction and scope of a company over a long span which translates into an advantage for it through its utilization of resources in a challenging market to meet its objectives (Whittington 28). Bryson (15) defines strategy as a pattern of purposes, policies, programmes, actions, or resource organization that clearly determine what an organization does, and why it does it. In all these definitions, there are some common strands of strategy that can be used to summarize what it is about. It is viewed as a long term activity which seeks to utilize resources available to position the organization in a competitive market situation. In essence it is a long term approach to implementing a company's business plans in an already challenging business environment.

The centrality of a strategy for every business has led to the application of different approaches to achieve the main objectivity. The recent financial constraints on most economies have necessitated implementation of creative ideas from the long tried and outdated models of cut-throat competition. Any discussion on business strategy must thus factor in these new approaches to give a sense of wholeness to its analysis. The business strategists have the leeway to chose from any new models of laying strategies as long as it suits their companies. The bottom line in laying the strategy must be the recognition of an opportunity when it arises. However the action taken should not be knee jerk but must arise from an already set course of action which is referred to as a business plan. The new model that most businesses are trying out is called the blue ocean approach. This is contrasted to the old approach of stiff competitive tactics to create profits and in this case, it is referred to as the red ocean strategy. The two terms were first used by W.Chan Kim and Renee Mauborgne in their business book, *Blue Ocean Strategy.*

The two terms, *Blue* and *Red Ocean* are coined from the precept that the business universe is made up of two kinds of space, red and blue. The red oceans are representative of the already existing markets and market players. Their business practices are well known and the industrial boundaries are clearly set and accepted. This ocean is also beset by competition whose rules are clearly understood (Chan 24). The lack of new demand amidst the stiff competition for existing demand eventually results in lower profits and growth hence the ocean is reddened as the competition increases even further. The red ocean aspect has come to spawn what is called the competitive business strategy. The strategy involves understanding the competitive forces, their underlying causes, thus revealing the sources of the company's profitability over time. The main competitive forces that shape a business include the threat of new entrants, bargaining powers of suppliers and buyers, the threat of substitute products and services and rivalry among existing competitors (Porter 28). All the forces are interconnected but the implication in all them is that they result in more competition which every company tries to beat. The strategy is grounded on trying to beat off the competitors in the face of falling demand and profitability. The innovations that might be incorporated are simply geared towards achieving this.

On the other hand, the blue ocean space denotes the markets that are not yet in existence. It includes the unknown or unexploited market space where profitability can still be achieved easily. The difference in strategy lies in the fact that demand is not fought over but rather created. The modern market world provides very many new avenues where opportunities can be harnessed to achieve sustainable profitability. These unexploited markets are referred to as the blue ocean as they are less prone to unnecessary competition. There is more calm and ample space to spread rapidly. For a company to return maximum profitability with the current economic slowdowns, the blue ocean strategy seems to be the best gamble. However, like all business practices, it calls for bold actions on the side of the company. The underlying implication still remains creating new opportunities through creating uncontested market space thus making the competition irrelevant. The assumption that companies have to compete within a certain given industry's structural condition as indicated in the competitive based strategies thus proves null and void (Chan 25). New market boundaries are broken to create the blue oceans through research. Some of the methods that a strategist can use to unlock boundaries include looking across strategic groups within existing industries, or across alternative industries among others (Chan 20). The underlying factor in blue oceans is restructuring what is already there instead of using it the way it is. The markets are thus restructured as per the plan that the company has set up to ensure resources will no longer be wasted trying to keep away competition. Creation of blue oceans gives rise to new brands that are unique and target a hitherto ignored market segment. The strategy is also not hinged on new technological techniques but utilizes what is already there to carve a niche.

In essence, the two strategies can be incorporated. A company can still fight for its niche but still create blue oceans within its larger structures; companies like Microsoft have survived due to successive creation of blue oceans in the face of onslaughts from its competitors. The current business environment calls for a strategy that is less costly and will ensure sustainable profit making. The blue ocean is the answer to the current saturation of the market and falling demand.

Works Cited

Bryson, J. *Strategic planning for public and nonprofit organizations: A guide to strengthening and sustaining organizational achievement.* San Francisco: Jossey-Bass Publishers, 2005.

Chan, K. Blue Ocean Strategy. *Harvard Business Review* , 210, 2005.

Porter, M. E. The five competitive forces that shape strategy. *Havard Business Review* , 79-83, 2008.

W.Chan Kim, R. M. *Blue Ocean Strtaegy:How to Create Uncotested Market Space and Make the Competition Irrelevant.* New York: Harvard Business School Publishing, 2004.

Whittington R, S. *Exploring Corporate Strategy, 8th Edition,.* Essex,: FT Prentice Hall, 2008.